simmering of a declarative void

Robert Kiely

Published 2020 by the87press
The 87 Press LTD
87 Stonecot Hill
Sutton
Surrey
SM3 9HJ
www.the87press.com

ISBN: 9781916477483
Design: Stanislava Stoilova [www.sdesign.graphics]

SPRING WINTER WHATEVER

the seasons are dead

        only a metallic screeching

                the fifth season's violins, autonomy's autumn

when the sun

        for an hour

                winds up the daffodils

and we go

        to ventilate evil

                which imports

                        this, today

sun

        on a dead

                page

the Amazon delivery number is squeezed onto my face
and love bears it to the edge of doom
and you only swipe once
fraught with the exact – we're
all pushing for non-alienated labour to
become alienated! like, don't cook *just eat*, free
delivery is why we shop there,
the televisual chair, so handsome, the
inappropes lol sounding really dodge and
doing the awkward turtle, in the hour of
need, catch
                    what's running   out

a hot bullet-hole | pooing a hollow hand clap
forced into Art's autonomy: loot this
negative frequency-dependent sexual selection
tube, the adjudication of source-churn and demand
in a groove of the lewd
snacking amidst woe
curtailed, with flares
plus a facial *trompe l'oeil* chin concealing a second food-hole
agitating for the amendment of
night falling like a plate | and broke
a fucking mess   hope

fetish-loot and jibes, barbed in the mind
snapchat holla'd at on faces of
gurning, *you fucking bevelled skeuomorph*
spider-silk in throwback catapult anachronism
on an infinite conveyor belt of compassion

from a pavement splattered tendons
a face eaten making it difficult to see or read or function
out of lava-flow:

                    eat me no more
    for I am thin to the point of

kiss from a distance with hyperextended tongues,
then skullfuck, turn most of you into a tympanum
trepanned and bleeding, brain spores over-eating
and spreading, forming soft dough for kneading

and the words admit they like it,
getting jerked off by a phantom limb
a real flatterer

                and thoughts

                in tension

                keep trim

disappearing as a hack
trace, wood chop, big sock all
over a Muybridge grid

which encapsulates space in crescendo,
suffusing the noosphere of the nearest Tesco

these the means
of a raw quintessence, tight lipped to slip a trick:
but none more quietly – a long grey landscape into the way it is
made out in a tiny subliminal signal

                And words go splattering, all silver

the gaps turn into panic scratching
wing-clipping
chewing the cheek off fate, observing
risk in a slow-mo spin

    the lightness fills the bathtub
    beware the water of the kettle   into the
    mines, mete want, some part of heart –
    to decide to shaft some sunlight

elsewhere a faded zenith postulated
in these lines: oft times not fully present
but sniffling and craning out of *here, now*

DIRECTOR: there might not be
anywhere else, another conversation worth
having

    the eye meets
    a regurgitating brook
    of schematics

    come to the end

try to cross my eyes
and dot each tease

the stars discharging or whatever
                              radical relaxation
yet   the whole
income months itself and houses you
all curiosity-defective, we up precaution
and it solicits ... yeh

crack it and peek inside

long sinewy

the sad fact is
it wants to impress
to the hilt

                                                                     it is

                                                                     a loss

                                                                     of nerve

HICCUP

Everybody is simply trying to be noncommittal.

So call resounds *no home* within a threaded bare

account to the bank of a river, servers twisted

through a public ovoid which some would

sue – which *works* and so *does not work*, spinning

a hamster-wheel pinned to a treadmill of no

cardio – annul the fascism stitched irrevocably

into over there, little machines whirring

in every corner, you exit your breakfast through

the vestibule, walled up visual field of dimethyl-

tryptamine pure – wrangle this from a brick of shit.

Blog unrivalled spirit-sequencing, the squeeze
                    is everything to all.

KILLING THE COP IN YOUR HEAD

cold arcs square down to juts   i clash sleep
to streams,, clouds gliding view

and scutter (plop)
                    falling out of   the catchall
vocab frying to only

say what say physics   they will know it

        by entrails   climbing frost

The scene is as follows. Interviewer sits at a desk. Guest sits across from him. Visible between them is a chessboard stuck to the wall. It has magnetized pieces and is mid-game. There is a bonsai tree to the left. It stands motionless throughout. The guest asks anxiously, fast, what is it we feel the need to scream into and who made it and where and when and for what purpose and under what kind of duress also known as working conditions and what was the rate of pay, what song on repeat has etched a new neural pathway with a ramp on it which a skateboarder who has spent the last hour or so scoping out the surrounding area kickflips off of and fails to land it, nutting himself. The interviewer nods. Once. Concomitantly, for the exact duration of the nod, which is brief, there is applause.

A sensation of restraint.

receding, one goes, like:: assertion 1 jumps off the tallest
building nearby,

negotiation won't sit with you at the lunchtable, tittering///
hyper throat-feelz

all the other speech-related adjective cum nouns acting hell,
a disc

scratched across///

pole to pole hop uh

The audience has a questionnaire about the performance they witnessed shoved under their nose. They ponder who exactly told them about the piece, or whether they saw it advertised, and where, and, more to the point, they ponder its impact on them as its consumer. This takes time and effort. Picture an artwork whose impact is total and self-evident to everyone it encounters. An artwork that gets its consumers to rate it 10 or 0, nothing in-between, on a scale of 0 to 10 for everything on the Arts Council questionnaire. The bonsai tree is silent. The artwork hits a demographic that is the perfect microcosm of the population within a ten-mile radius of its performance, always. Imagine an artwork that conscripts its audience and forces them to return to it again and again and wants them to understand the whole world through it. It burdens them with an interpretive and imaginative labour when fuck that. It asks them to work for free. It asks them to evangelize it to their mates and crowdfund its sequel and keeps growing even when they look away. No longer a possibility, the artwork becomes sentient and applies for its own funding. There is applause. This is the paperclip problem in the realm of aesthetics. Artificial stupidity. Who speaks. Its blue plaque is unveiling everywhere. They fold the questionnaire 103 times and then the *merely* prises open a small gap at which point their agency is meekly inserted. Then they all go through their whole life never speaking of it for the simple reason of a blackmail note from the origin itself which reads *Imma fuck you up anyway but you want this to be quick or slow?*

expanse of   no apathy

kindling to a clipped drop

too late   levelling   singular this

coarser movement

There is still applause. The majority of our lives are an exegesis of the First Epistle to the Thessalonians 4:11.

Acephalic roaches are capable of living for weeks. Humans, however, would bleed to death. The human body cannot eat without the head, the body would die from starvation. The bonsai tree is silent. Primitive neopterans breathe through spiracles, or little holes in each body segment. The spiracles pipe air directly to tissues through a set of tubes called tracheae, no central authority. Insects have clumps of ganglia equally distributed within each body segment capable of performing the basic nervous functions responsible for reflexes, so without the brain, the body can still function in terms of very simple reactions. They can stand, react to touch and move. The head is fine, waving its antennae back and forth for several hours until it runs out of resources.

reassembling in all lost the the daily bust of car-crashed
        glass living in a room
barely able to //the real thought which stops and goes, stops
        and goes,   both
feet all the way down on the accelerator and brake,

Applause. the way out runs screaming into the forest,

assertions 10 through 20 are playing russian roulette

The course will grow between the arrows of our intentions.
Mould.

The room is empty. There is a couch, a bed, a table with two chairs, a kitchenette, and an ensuite. There is also a closet, and many other objects. The duvet on the bed is without a cover. Its white is browning. Rapidly. One bit of it bursts into flame. An unused TV sits in the corner. The day outside. The window is sunny. It is unclear what floor we are on. The tabletop is also darkening in its centre. It is quite far from the duvet. Black smoke is colouring the white ceiling. The tabletop spouts flames too. Repeat for every object. It is unclear whether the sun is setting or the windows are simply darkening from the smoke.

under that shrink and safety blanket   gash the bucket,

dependency as a cut   decision striated with   and

we need. so unsure. we is they from the beginning of the

earlier draft   be pulled worse than teeth, every line bursts

cut shut// trapped free

Orthorexia. Applause. Assertions. Their bodies piled.

raw interpassivity. Each city is a sleeping superorganism.

FIGURATIVE POEM

content exceeds rage
defaults the rent,
needs the next adage
to kick in from the boundary
of forced closure

like: crash and shout
thrash a roue in cash
itch your rash

scrape the loud land and
dump it in the submission box
wound in cloth
        ~~kerosene~~

then: jilted hex turns to spurn all it learned
open-necked flex
to the hilt in jest
it burns to test itself
and nest from all the rest

then: the median freed decrees its need
and tramples the rest to brambles

leaves some dent
glinty
changed,
erased

like all justified the knots tied to lies frothing
in a tide

like really nearly
move yearly near to this fear
and leer, veering

but at a pace designated as *right* and it is   on the wing

senseless pinches of
salted violence
doled to those in holes
and never out of there

outside a gravy carriage down the lane
to hit the main vein
in a creche full of refs

who extend jumping ringworms
through the fire, with all the leopard slugs
mating before humans knew dangling

who enact a tax on all that lack
then flip with a grip to the long palm frond

the yellow marsh raves
stacks of history are laid out and rekindled
co-concrete the concerted rubble
waiting to be re-assembled in feathers

in the future to stare and see
someone from the past, but oblique, like
a homeless person you walk past every day
or shoo off an entry-way
ascending with a fresh haircut
a special gleam   all fair   all over
        careens the rut and fuss

SUCTION

consanguine we flick out to splits
pant   shallow, pane of stretched film, clinging

looks compacted, shatter to
tiny –   gravity pools whatness

propriety goes   plash
effaced then latticed into
                    sucked-in
a gaze is peeled off and out
and over   the give-in

THE ETHICS OF PRODDING

trust nothing especially your own
          implants   no   speech scrapes past lips   as if fury could
as if others could   as if some trace
                    of thought   hold back and halt   as if you just

preterite participation, nails gone
en mass, 'mergent and migratory

                                        we want   still

an object-clause in English gone
                              to a great sea

when i heard you had another hairpin
i smashed mine
and fucked its dust to the wind
shrieking to woo
but it doesn't work, anomie,
defeated by architectonics

they move in chronological hissing
the spires, cranes
insistent, like an election or traffic jam
        geographical lag
the topic sentence of exit   then   new vocabulary congeals, a
blood pudding strained through squealing, landing in tongues.
nerve-torn ‘twixt a giant wallet and a ladder up a waterfall,
    to distract from or acknowledge
    the baying mob always baying

selfies in secret state bunkers

crime   what it is   and how to commit it

HOW TO READ

They don't tell you about the gravity of inertia, its infinite history.

frozen inside

bullshit   like pearls apparent

this woozy song in faux-zen :

We are astride Maslow's hierarchy of needs, which like a pyramidal rubix cube in a tricky gif is shifting, and we get each sensation as it, well, I'm not sure how, or what the criteria are, but basically you sometimes feel fulfilled and self-actualized while starving and lonely, or have a sense of belonging while feeling unsafe, etc.

Ideas congregate first, etched onto paper then built around what's there. People go up and down escalators and don't congregate until a structure is built to do so and occupied from 8am to 7pm by the well-dressed then 9pm to 7am by people crawling on hands and knees scraping crumbs, the building's roots are capital flows.

debt decides all

debt whispers its tonality

with no interest

generations each

successively leaning

on the next

squeezing legions

fall is zoom

stitched to your skull

and leeched

old horses housed for nothing

    broken for nothing

sun   core

the sky's lid nears you

parallel lines

no animal has its place

it recedes

we get skinnier

wanderers never return

but make others older

swelling away

maybe it was a distraction from what was
happening front-and-centre foreground,
                    we were straining backstage

anyway   look back and you're gone
cracked into the wall
confiscated and shredded

those who are missing, those who disappear
and resurface   bizarrely refashioned

frozen in 1884 or 1920 or 1956 or 1966 or 1967or 2016 or
        2019

seconds BANG hours BANG days BANG

you who are missing, or returned as ghosts:
        we do not ask you what really happened
        we wake screaming through no mouth
        we gnaw to your hunger

                to speak is to spit the clot in your
                mouth, to spit the clot is to raise a
                fist, is to prove you exist
                        to spit pure denial

circulate this counterfeit

in truth   every hair retracts

to consult a tongue-split

somnambulist   this bill

of infinite goodwill

warmth   and sincerity

holding it   in check

my mooring is mist and zoos

and with no sunset i roll on

the sky bends buildings

an asteroid is no clarity

three-quarter moon fixed sky, frost towards it

flows sleep / foam-lights

Hong Kong is no church

it is morning in Calgary and LA, evening in Cork

cargo is in the blood, blood

        in the cargo

You build a bridge and then you burn it. You build a bridge and then you burn it. You build a bridge and then you burn it because you have to relocate. You build a bridge and then you burn it because of a war. You build a bridge and it is shut down because the economy tanks and the maintenance cost is too high and then it is burned. You reopen another bridge where the same thing happened before. But it didn't burn. You build a bridge and then you burn it. You build a bridge and then you bury the workers who built *that* bridge in the foundations of the *next* bridge and you burn the last bridge and don't talk about that bridge anymore, no one does. The new bridge is good though. You build a bridge and then you burn it because they're sending nothing worthwhile your way. You build a bridge and then you burn it. You build a bridge and then they burn it. You cross a bridge. You discover an old untouched bridge, you can't believe it. You discover this old untouched bridge and everything about this bridge is fine and it needs no maintenance, weirdly. You cover the bridge up again because you have to move. The physical land you're occupying moves elsewhere and that bridge isn't there anymore. They build a bridge and then you burn it. You build a bridge and then you burn it. You switch sides. You build a bridge and then you burn it. You build a bridge and then you burn it just because. The bridges are out of use. You forget what bridges are for. You think they are for burning. You burn the bridge because you think they might burn the bridge first. It's ridiculous, but there it is.

renounce the life you have planned

the boomerang strapped to your back
                                                            pings

then there are echoes

all this talk's not-naught yet fixed

            in place with a firing pin

concrete, old poems

word tunnels

the stroke of

your favourite character

pissing on the sun

the mail held back

      laptop infected

the climate controlled

a state
          seeing bee-white

released   into

burst   bubble

no-one is good

eyes   cracked

  soul   is a dog

to which i am allergic

  give me   a bump

meanwhile they jafted by the window

they spoke of an award for contribution

but no opportunities could be discerned

and the centrifuge filched it

back for some // voluntarism

and the degrees of its hold

balancing over-involvement and avoidance

huge nuts duck through fluffy courts

words constructed this harbour but won't

maintain it, estate agents treat edgeland

artists to tea and biscuits

this is not a loss //

end your tract vaguely for more volunteers

as it's being slurped up

they weren't trying to insult and they ordered

riding a discourse they cannot plunge

no *pinned* to the present

five eighths of the time a dropped pin

tells them all they need

to know, zooming out fully to see

three of them

a funeral for the living

all taken all monitored

indifferently yet rage inoculation

as form-filling

equations tarmacadaming the future

tectonic plates a momentary inconvenience

price everything as if it is the last

imperative to reply sealed in

a glass bottle

eyes duct-taped to the exhausted

canary in the mine and the mine

is a metaphor for, like, the future and stuff

increasingly one feels less over

a larger surface area

crisp as one would never see

in all combinations and modified

for purchasing parity

cut along the cusp of the mind

what once was metal

is foam in the when and now

something missing, dreaming

a quiver of ill time

in the here and then

knowing both sides, fence-laden

didn't help

anyway this engine, thought, its horrid fuel

its straining

against its basis

relentless, knarled stump

root to death

flattening to the usual

unfurling at cost

vine minus trunk

plus drought

The wail is in your marrow. Fuck stars. Strip back. Cram in a man, line up some lambs to flourish; their law is up against the wall. All flops down to the low accretion of coral.

The weight of history always converges on a knife-edge. It is not all-pervading but discrete, it is not subtle but taut. It is pain, cuts ties. Look, in the beginning were the minutes of the previous meeting. In the end there were resolutions. Implementation is up to another universe.

We shall die, these bodies will fail and these words with them, and never return, never, and that equally this moment will forever have been, that we will have shared it and never be able to feel otherwise for eternity, that at this very moment your eyes pass over this very word and lose sight of the last, or if you are being read this, that each phoneme comes and obliterates the last and they pile high in mind only.

The world demands elongation. This pitch could only ever be delivered as if the investors were always already in. They weren't.

Clammy declamatories. The tendency is to end on the smoothed out, patted down truism.

The Phillips Economic Analog Computer is filled with a red liquid.

I can't finish.

The rest of the city doesn't sleep but that doesn't *change* anything, it is plagued by bad acting flavoured with water and a lack of professionalism, swimming in immanence, there is total silence, all the sea is dying.

sit useless and dead

crowd proven

progress reaping sleaze

tired they tend to zen

oh fair doctor, racy and killing the board

placed into lard jets

kind calm call is ever

as first to worst

vying with

the azure

standing under

confusion

SPECULUM TENDRIL

for Nisha Ramayya

let neglect this wide lens, or

so the Aryans go down by osmosis
and render the monkey-god subjugate, itself stretched
by Brownian motion to and from what we now
call China,
and the patchwork tatters, there never were
any tribes

but the monoliths of, um, old... for good reason —

from there it is dragged forward
by the leash while trying to shit
until the pads of the feet come off

them pointy ears still got it

raucous, a deep-fried map

is spliced into someone

whose happiest moment was this one time

skydiving through the Andes and realizing

he had seen just this in Planet Earth season

three, knowing we are all in this rerun:

it doesn't matter what we *think*.

to be jolted in blue

to imitate an inexplicable logic

wrapped in irrelevance

moon-stained, carving away
at the extraneous, too small

and cold.

loving malignancy

rust bursts fast

and old parts replay

with then without love and children

conspicuous, unbidden

down to the roots

APPLES

In this tiniest of musk oxen all balled up
amongst these blunt lobstacles in a cup
with a soundclown
eating this ream of
double Gloucester down
driving around town
with mint cats.
MINT. CATS.

We won some scat
and a glass of biscuits.
The door breaks and you fix it.

My every character-flaw returns to me now,
Bigger, and with more facepaint.
In getting older (and bigger)
the highs get higher and
the lows get lower. That is to say,
I am now taller.

APOPHATIC

Temp 1 and Temp 2 fight
it out
for the job and then:
This is building to the
fearsome subcommittee
undermining their own
minuting
with keyhole-text-surgery
nanobot-like results
some serendipity
dancing to a timelapsed
circumflex
let everything in swim
encapsulated by a transgressive
car-park rooftop
hemihelix
perfectly square clouds
wild and timid
collapsing trips to
flotillas, viewed from an
unenterable toilet brim
and hand-eye coordination
no inheritance
disinterred to arrive
Emptying the bin
by inversion
glimmers shrill the sink
jawsongs
dyed in skips (
a Mobius dick
That for example one is angry then not
rescued from the teeth of a dream

risk dispersal as contagion
the third eyeing up the
familiar reference points
collapsing at short notice in a torrent of self-
congratulation. The exchanges squeezed out
of a tedious reaming.
Bursting into the thing I
tend to repeat in poems,
as if working it out
with a stencil or spirograph
but it is more like how
the smoke *sees* (
skinlike paper, formaldehyded previous employees
blanks are getting their outline
traced. All the words have been spoke
, now scream

TINSEL SHUFFLE ROT

Inside the sky, a spectrum-shift. Wax figures beneath.
The poem so far has covered desolation, the biology
Of fat, and mothers. In what follows, the poem will
Cover intellectual property, the hollow of your eyes, and
Transformation. On the train, someone reads *Homo Deus*
    and someone
Else reads *The Sound and the Fury* and someone else
Reads the *Evening Standard* and someone else reads
Between the World and Me and someone else reads some
Audre Lorde. One's indeterminate needs to be updated ASAP.
Please notice. It is 2017. Abandonment issues gallop across the
Normal. Inside the sky, ash. Here and there, a plane. The
    wax is much
Too realistic. The veins, the exposed teeth, integrity shot to shit.
Afropessimism, Conservativism, and mornings have been
    covered by
Now. Another is watching *Manhattan*, another is eating
Spring rolls. Everybody keeps going to work.
Correction, most people keep going to work.
Correction, work keeps coming to some people.
There is no horizon. There are flat-earthists. In union,
This the completeness of no shoes. Domestic industry and
Domestic workers in the foundations experience no overlap.
It is bare missing word. This is a disposition to iniquity.
The dust in the architect's dream. Stop moving.
Everything keeps getting easier. The bad
And the good. Independently. The restructure goes
On and new roles open up. Someone retracts the
Donation of their body for medical research.
In the restructure everyone's face will be superimposed
And each aberration smoothed out. Things rattle
Around inside their names. Correction, not everyone.

But more than a few. Less than everyone and
More than a few. The catharsis of the correct
Analysis lies down across the sky. Some people on
The train are not reading. In other warnings on
Sunk capital food is consumed. For example,
Ghost chillies. The retraction came too late,
Hence the screaming. It is the year of the resurgence of
Cancelled. In what follows, you can expect endings over
And over. It has covered nominalism and Woody Allen so far.
The anoriginary buttress must be accommodated, busted
Or switched. Fixed-rates on oseophagal massages with
        mini-guillotines,
Working wonders on malpraxis. Look, we can de-scribe or
        we can
Re-script. Can we prescribe the spectrum from the triangulated
Node purely inferred? Who locked who out? Who locked
        who in?
Who locked what in where? The passives fail to elide
The problem. Rupert Murdoch's hair. The skin fans
Out to reveal nerves and lymph. Yellowed. The tongue
Arching out and each layer visible of what lies beneath the
Street and leech. It isn't clear what many of the passengers
Are reading if on Kindles. A vast amount
Of material is repeatable. Things are trapped on the
Escalator that is their names, gradually smeared over the
Grill. There are degrees. There are degrees of progress and
        there
Are degrees of heat. The snow is weak. The unsunk capital
Traipses with a lightness that leads to a jolting then expunged
Shock. There are degrees of knowledge. There are degrees
Of distance and of sleep. Someone else stares at nothing.
The mirror flattens the wax figure which didn't flatten any
Thing. There are degrees of hate. Turned
To the side, the line-lengths follow closely

Our recent sales figures in the first quarter.
It isn't too good of a thing to be
Too splayed. Down in the margins
And across to hands held in breach
Of the loss. Anemones of the cloud
By light's beginning dim. Drawn between
The surface and manual, crushed. It is not 657.
There is a calculus to tasks and their
Settings out and off. It does not take
Any force for it to be so smooth. No,
Retract. The tweaks are so disheartening but
To get it right the first time doesn't happen.
There are degrees of love. Activity of the
Breakdown harnessed in infinite deferral of
Defeat. It seems fixed too easily and the
Modifications trail off. People listen to
Black social death as they jog. This is an
Inquisition on sublimity. Someone bursts into
Tears on a bus. This is an execution of fecundity.
They who precede the ranks in the possession-form
Earlier make less sense now. Outside the sky there are
No available seats. Someone breaks a window on a train.
There is no home. Levels of agitation groan. The actors and
Agents do casting calls unseen. There is no free zone.
So far the poem has covered travel, investment, and
Summaries. And then the columns tear down from the
Sky a portcullis. This is the exoneration of infinity. The purple
And green bleed into each other. A missed putt transpires to be
Non-symbolic. Worldwide limnic eruption of no hoard.
It is not 2897. The stock exchange but in wax. The godhead is
Deaf. The name doesn't coincide with anything at all. The
Wick goes down too fast. Someone else is fiddling fingers and
Someone else is listening to Robin Williams and someone else is
Listening to William Basinski. The questions were a decoy.

Correction, there are no hands but wings. Correction,
sometimes
It is right. Surreptitiously. *It must stop*. Freeze one for later.
Aggregate individual yearnings make monstrosity. These
children were
Told a random combination of fantasy, outright lies and simple
Truth, all in the same tone of voice. The updates come through
And so it starts again. Beside the sky, red-shift. Someone
Retracts the donation of their library. Some things keep moving
Backwards. There is no pillow. On the boat, someone reads
Emma
And someone else reads *Harry Potter and the Prisoner of
Azkaban.*
The song has so far enveloped dissolution, cancer, and futurity
Itself. Wax candles starboard. The wick is unburned. It is
Just in time. This is a condensation of obliquity. It is
Damaged very readily and tapers off. The forms
Have language that breaks them, renders them
Invisible to administrators. The lawn is an
Improvisation. Decoagulation of the backhand
Management. There are pedigrees of lateness.
It is too much to be frayed. The walls are lined with
Specimens. Most diseases imaginable, most abstractions
Such as age are represented for each. You imagine that
Your organs will remain with you, unaugmented.
One needs fuel in a way which elaborates on
The contingencies linking the criteria on the set-page, threading
And building muscle between the sedimentations forced into a
Narrative skeleton. This is how it is done. Arabesque veins
decorate
The museum. Students study nearby. There are lists of phone
Extensions and the ways to forward and intercept calls propelled
Forward to a warning of what will come. Undetected particles
Fall on the blueprint. The distinction between needs and wants is

Absolutely central to an economic system which allocates
Resources in apparently-efficient ways. Like an explosion with
The know-how of all the world's engineers, architects, and builders.
The viewpoint should be clearer but diminishingly isn't. For example,
You *want* to continue to function at what might be designated a physically
And mentally healthy level. You *need* to keep in mind that this is not a need.
Attempted corrections are counterproductive. Shit flows down
The Thames. Risen capital lopes at the margins. This is the perdition
Of contingency. Move less. Traditional practices fumigate the
Mausoleum. The ekphrasis of a subjective catachresis sleeps
In the ground. Passengers circulate. There are pedigrees of cheese.
This poem was written in late 2017 in London. Make it irrelevant
Please. Get to know your needs. The sky underneath bare feet.

SILLY JISM

And foremost premise (d) the tripling sores deliver (c) trifling
promise of a boat w/ the dock pacing the hills (b) termination and the mountains
cresting skylines
brought to the foundation of (a) presidential premise that each hoop jumped
is a haptic antiseptic
jammed into a septum petty (b) assertion insects bite my sleep and so
(c) derivation is that the bourgeoisie have only two senses, entitlement and propriety but it
transfers back to the premise hidden behind the trifling promise over the first line break like a heat transfer or a
money transfer or a room transfer or an energy transfer, or (a) presumed transfer of funds or an electron transfer
and that is a problem like a problem-child or a health problem, or a problem-case or a drug problem or a drink
problem or the transition problem or this next tiny premise

(b) a grime comet as the approximate prospects
of improvement which are impersonated
by a full body cleanse for the chakras
of an elongated legless pug, i.e. trout
and then
an ovary
circluding
a sperm
containing us as (d) executive premise with the rhetoric of responsibility or a case of the pot calling the
departing kettle back to apologise with an (e) paltry premise, such as oh you know in time models became
sclerotic unto utter uselessness so (b) suppository you return to the womb and find you're over-qualified in
regal contortionist dross/ tinned swag/ scar tissue
have been destroyed and reassembled, destroyed and reassembled, destroyed and reassembled
on repeat

BATS

this bat is named
do not kill pets
when the food goes away
what do you have
what
will you take
hunting a shape-shifting
road sign
from the doorframe
creaking
in the mountains
which cancel
the seas
the lakes
cancelled
by the hills
trees
by roots
birds
by slugs
hawks
by maggots
imagine
the third person
over there
in a cage
the cage
cancelled
by the surround
that person
cancelled by
imagine

the second person
and that person
by the
first person
cancelled by
imagine
the null person

we were a small stone cottage
at a gate
having our signs defaced
by twelve men in hunting livery
rat-catcher attire
then we were the spray paint
amending the tolls
the fines
then we were the ladder they were using
then their shoes

those hands
drape your shoulders
like bags of blood
the arm
broken
at the elbow
reaching out

elsewhere, children torn to donkeys
or in a still life
being made to sit
for five years

these people
touch the problem

then jump
into the
swamp
to get
something obscure
at one level
as a relation
embodied
practiced
honed
isolated events
in a prism
a point of view
fearful wings
control
the agency of the object
asked
to rationalize itself
it flips out
the window

no admittance
but a break
for emergency
access
only
to undo
the great injury
of now
not with
agility but
slow and brute force

the prime mover

in all its regalia
here it is
simply moveable
like a squeeze of the
wrist
just never leave me
no pulse
and the crawling
to resist
an ulcer
to tonic sheets of brined skin
and sure they are
moving fast
me to them
them to me
to avoid being food

there is no such thing
as a city of the immortals
there are no immortals
but goons in balaclavas
heavies
with a British van
outside 34 North Frederick Street
the occupants, torn

owning
is the application of angle grinders

they flit between empty houses
and electron-fizz
in the dusk

my words are vacant
it is difficult
to imagine
circumstances different
to exactly these
I write process documents
so that anyone
can do it
so that tomorrow
a temp can come in
and have no excuse
like simple poems
where a poet can walk in
and there's no excuse

what I mean
is something about
administrative labour
and simplicity and directness
the point being
about what happens
before you get in the door
maybe when
that building's foundations were laid
but also not
that it is lost
in advance
what I meant
I said imperfectly

the poem is not simple
it is complicated
like getting around
the town or country
or between
is complicated
I wish I could
enumerate how
but I can't count higher
than seven
and sometimes that seven
is like the upper
part of an irrational
fraction

the ingredients
were mushed up
in the cream
then poured onto a plate
and cold-fried
then she scraped them up
into rolls
and put them
in a cup
a desperate artisanal
present in regress
from passive
to active
the skills like shells removed

I used to think
the saying and the doing
were separable
nothing in particular
needs to be said
though much
needs to be done
but that only works
if you cut yourself off
as an individual
like you are you
it's untenable
see how far
it goes

I write through to its end
the brutal core
which I read care
for example
when people from smaller islands
visit bigger islands
they often feel
there are too many people
and it is too busy
and they get tired
and return home
this is called
ethnography

no longer personal
but still private
an advert is
for what happens anyway
like quantum fizz
or damage
this form
stamped by buffalo
there is no life
it is signed by infrastructure
there are no buffalo
and in the possible
nothing happens

you look out the window
and see some greenery
a unit
it is measured
it has a distinct
health benefit
and the callipers come down
who holds them
the callipers
what holds them
the ridges
the ligaments

at work they have pay grades
the grades contain spines
you move up the spine
if you perform well
but you don't move up grades
for performing well
this is to prevent
promoting people to incompetence, i.e.
you're good at doing this, so
you are kept doing that
you understand
you get a gold star
on your forehead

it goes past all that
understanding miles of ghosts
in empty refrains
it is not this or that beautiful
there is a certain kind
there is a certain kindness
in the cut in pulling at that edge
sometimes things just get blown up
with difficulty sometimes
in a trifling manner
and crawled have back at it
without a way through
other than the angle of the magnetic
field against the horizon

it is the familiar feel of the rug

suddenly taken from overhead

and stitched into your pool

revoking the permanent

        frosted glass

is no dwarf-order

the skips cancelling

        or moving backwards

to the Neolithic multispecies resettlement node

            the symbiotic outgrowth

sandwiched or smoked

a spider huddles in the cold

    indistinguishable from its web

        planar and ashen

there are absolutely no holes
in creation, your neck is
a sinew, your head
a balloon animal

invited to the quality
committee, you tend the bonsai
in the court (of slaughter)

the era of the sun-holiday is over, localized
entirely in the global Northwest
and our
sum-opacity is where people state plainly *I have
lost friends to lesson-planning*
+ that is the camber of the road
where the road
stands in for our orientation to the future,
that road
which used to bear a different name depending
on the way you walked it
a different name again if you crawled it
and always
always depended on your destination laughing
against the prow at the door

I've had to go to work today, in a long keypad
stepping lock up to the kind of simple but glad
reaction of being dressed and on time
in the correct clothes, not quite a necktie
affair

        counting down on the table, misted with stain
ventriloquizing doesn't paint
brightly but lunges through like bratwurst
plated and rotating, the stickers which hurt
too much so undo the beholding of this turgid vein

                                                    risk it, strategic
nonchalance of gaming this massive
                                                transcendental
precondition of our lips press accidental
onto the screen, mistaking the image's lick

for the chemical classification of disintegration
        , glabrous marginalia treated as instruction
for this here satyr, peddling the wares
of unconscious prayers, the grotesque
notebooks of youth and forced sanitation

in puny blocks, assemble, like on a bicycle
        I see stretching out a skyscrapéd oracle
in money flows, the dyed binary code
floating over needy heads
it's a conceit, sure, but not at all intangible
            margins centred on insectoid senses

immense pawn shops, defunct motivations
like a clod of glitter without a theory
a vile nexus
murdering every murmur
as if it went down
a tangent again

it can't be done anymore
it simply looks
like this, now
every deixis is without a theory
a false silence, corroded but
the slack it gives
cannot be doubted
in its invisible employment
except for the gases
in the room,
it's difficult to imagine
whose tongue falling back whose throat
to spite whose sense of
bodily autonomy
a fluke in the sonic

sing the granularity
of the spring swelling
I'm not sure anyone
understands the effect they have
or what it is
to say: no more of that
calming
sea, addressed to me
quintupled in snow without a theory
for the scapegoat of the throat in the simmering
of a declarative void
folded clothes calculating
an iris-twitch clasping without a theory this finger

the absolute limit of
the hedgerow
calmed down an astrolabe
of contempts to be hurt to be hurt
without a theory
of hurt getting used to
all of them having the same name
I am a source of danger and must be safeguarded against
smudged bodies
putting whatever you want in it
threading the ribbon without a theory
through a needle   it rasps
in the dream, the greasy veneer
to repulse
every day every day a new one every day
it adds up don't it
which is the
syntactically last mathematical procedure
the railroad of goo
in your visor   sounds repeated three
the scripts are split
to their fish-fine rats
neglected nearest might in scorning
I try to read it but it is too close leaping lock or key
intersected employee number, train ticket and login hiss
can you not play with your food here it is not even my name
I see the manager, to work out
my complicated feelings
as if I could locate my feeling
in some locus of statements, as if not fizz
prompting voiceovers

it is ventriloquism itself
speaks to you
asks for the secrets it whispered in distortion
and the colours revert, so easily
I like to imagine trees
since I have never seen one properly so-called
handed the words for objects classified or out of commission
like songs you learn only on leaving;
there are numbers like
scratch and pentacle
hardly thrown without a theory of
pre-arranged networks of legitimization
collapse
into a call directed at no-one
it isn't anything like that at all
moving from one room to another just for the different sounds
this improvised heartbeat
and cairns cutting the horizon
I know they are real   would
you spill blood en route some would

suck this organizational or administrative-value
claiming to start sentences with "I truly believe cover
and personal freedoms
are family values to punish weasel words"
*where are the innocent*s someone asks,
voice-throw-overplaid into the batter-mix
to occupied character cognition without a theory of character
or pain
plasticizing the sediment
and wishing width was different
it is impossible of course
for the flowers to bloom
at the wrong time
in quietist derision
no
don't listen
only listen
to the rubble
only listen
to the sea
and interpret loosely

of course, I have met my maker
our faces pressed up against the terrarium it was stormy outside
to add to that homely feeling this is important
flailing force of habit in a constellation
reconstituted with a softer accent
sitting in the corner just like so
and the rain
not trivial, like the sleet
would paw the rafters
if anyone had them
to be descending in a dream
twilight of the rising glue
of this afterlife
falling to skin
there are people without a theory out there and in here
who feel bad breaking even
for the right reason balanced on the flotilla
without a theory of the flotilla
without a theory
for falling in
without a theory
for flying away
or swimming

they will   immunize your eyes to night
they live   fastened inside barnacles
would blow up a set-piece presupposed and
would you spare a
lure aside the trail of ash eyes, to be imminently
pushed out from the back of the aggregate
head
the errata without a theory
of ringing the doorbell and running
to sell insurance for
ballets of obsolescence vestigial organs of perception
to cloud forms and

inside the pain of the dream is the waking consideration
would you   haltingly
dressed as the manager of my manager
inside their ear-piece on the stage as the extra who
plays almost every non-leading role
and signs away the rights
and never hears how it was used
for a theory of posterity
behind the fronts of their eyes
like double-denim
or a lisp

inside a neural sway a flare
sighs from the sidelines
that there of gripping the edges of the pool is so *unbecoming*
adaptation as concession
fluffing a blush without a theory
of the young scum
to peer down the rafters as if
the gallows fit
the vision of a squirrel
negotiating barbed wire
who speak unresolved windy forms
sown like cashews into a ladder   snips of charcoal
trodden underfoot
by an animatronic mammoth
we the dead nothing
have nothing to say   to us
blotched possibilities
in the shade of a surpassed
season
could you even flatten your tongue enough
for our innate orientation
to light

lather up spontaneous combustion
to declare that assorted   box
and so it goes to die doubtless, support:
and then this radical door tries then locks
and they're jellified amongst them
all to get in a mooring like smilingly
the slinking untwists towards the cryptic
peace, throughout the land jumps for joyful hope,
boom,   back to the continental slope
no a line   up unless
to take away almost all over space
to structure the skyline to acquiescence,
chant stupidities in backscape,
though well-behaved irrefutably, should
tudor imperturbability make
you mean, put it back up, the fucking hood.

And then the seances swept down from the high-altitude lakes. The wagons were circled around the said, screaming threats at the birds going about their leisure. The pigmentation of the skirt was running no ran to the waves. Then everything was locked up, abstraxions vomited into neat little packaging then let's say logistics. The keys crumble into a fine or snap and so there is not any no no jut a way to venture. A voice over the intercom as an alarm be alarmed and you cannot close your ears. The crying runs right off water backs up the pipe. I pour out my life in the warm clingfilm of a space to be called for another year and then on a rolling basis home pour out the warmth for to be left alone with one other. Rise the jagged knife the roads acting like they'll last more than a year. Would shrink to sing low. An arcane hex of digits and python grips onto our eyes they are ours to this darkness of the present. The walls whisper the whisper is silence the silence is not a gap. Dwelling outside of the place where business is deemed to happen during the hours in questioning is ornament like the plastic moulding. The columns climb and I wish words conjured smells better. The topic at hand is something like ripples or human movement across all of space for let's say a limited time like a day. Somebody climbs the side of the building to adjust the sign, falls and dies. The patter of bodies. Your skin cracks even on your eyes is that skin you ask. What are these vendors why do we shrink and every lashing out turns to an in could we destroy directionality. This space's urgent reply. The words that would levitate gravel. All these distributed forms and refrains and rhymes to bear and break. Look it isn't this these processes written down to ensure we're all fireable the taste the way the straining terraforms the neck and shoulders its predictability balled up folded into surprise. The rates cut. The cut into a cap. The sky is just the colour of someone else's roof.

in the grotesquerie of the dream a mere grain of rice
locked in an immense vault
you know what's inside without a theory, and have to drill
anyway
contains the man on the train
distressed
trying to cut himself
with a bike chain fed up
blurs coordinate the banality
of that motif
and the plant rots, over-watered
sorry hello
on secondment then furloughed in fragile paper coffin
of lessons long forgotten

adjacent to prolonged
sun-damage
hanging a heaven-spent mirror it is so beautiful
because alone without a theory
and bouncy
breaking milestones
in torn hinges
in annotated antidotes
in curlews
and oystercatchers
dotting sand

IN IT

minds of air

they sit and stare

they sleep beneath their streams

a voice less terse

dwells in the furze

glossing political teams

the condensation gathers

on our mirrors

  forming a meniscus

for black mould

this serated look it glint and resting

just on the skin

can we this unplugged

grown to feed so low

in structures of body cold

the root fast-forward grow

I want to pick it

the scab

do you remember

being told

if you got the right job

you'd never work

a day in your life

yeah that

    amygdala level

    that is your enemy

a clipped wing

a toeless stub

the entire cosmology

of anti-pigeon spikes

the ways it makes

what it calls nature

adapt

where is it

what does it please

where is the outside

it's difficult to locate

my landlord is nervous when

we meet

at the centre of that nervousness

is a precious oil

I must extract

I keep thinking about it

the inversion of

the immiseration thesis

its sentiment a point

a fiction like all points

to produce the math of the everyday

which is the limit-case of the real math

another sentiment:

at a poetry reading, someone spoke

about their father, a prison screw

in a colonial conflict. Pick one.

He was executed by the other side.

They said, after a moment, "Maybe

he deserved to die."

Sometimes I wake up inside it.

Turn what we usually feel inside

out and you get close to it

let's be clear

there is a queen

she walks around

pick one

with her head and

neck connected

she walks or moves or

listen or

simple look

everything can be

a scalpel

there is a queen

there is calm

the head

the neck

a straight line

was extended from this infinitely small

point occupying no space

and swung about

it was not rigid, having no dimensions

the skin is just a series of transitions

to scattered probabilities

I crept up on them slowly

wearing a mask

and I saw a shadow or maybe a stain

        but I guess I'm calling your show to

ask what it was and how to sneak past it

          or inside of it

a crevice in its   just ride it

        out. I worked the skin from the flesh

with my flint, tendons flesh stringy

              in a garden I had achieved my goal

      I had a pet.

although dying

takes much time

and commitment

living

is something some of us

must do

My friends:

You are so much stronger

Than you even know.

ACKNOWLEDGMENTS

These poems or versions of poems have previously appeared in *datableed, Brexit: Borders Kill, Poetry Wales, Sure Hope, erotoplasty, MOTE,* and *York Literary Review*, among others. KILLING THE COP IN YOUR HEAD was initially published in a pamphlet by Sad Press, HOW TO READ by Crater Press, some of [a sequence] appeared as part of the Earthbound Poetry Series, and IN IT in a small run by Gang Press. My thanks to all the editors for their support.